Hard-headed Dinosaurs

Robin Birch

CHELSEA
CLUB HOUSE
An Imprint of Chelsea House Publishers

Chelsea Clubhouse
An imprint of Chelsea House Publishers
132 West 31st Street
New York, NY 10001

Chelsea Clubhouse books are available at special discounts when purchased in bulk quantities for businesses, associations, institutions, or sales promotions. Please call our Special Sales Department in New York at (212) 967-8800 or (800) 322-8755.

You can find Chelsea Clubhouse on the World Wide Web at: http://www.chelseahouse.com

First published in 2002 by
MACMILLAN EDUCATION AUSTRALIA PTY LTD
15–19 Claremont Street, South Yarra, 3141

Visit our Web site at www.macmillan.com.au or go directly to www.macmillanlibrary.com.au

Associated companies and representatives throughout the world.

Library of Congress Cataloging-in-Publication Data
Birch, Robin.
  Hard-headed dinosaurs / by Robin Birch.
  p. cm. — (Dinosaur world)
  Includes index.
  Summary: Describes the appearance, eating habits, and habitat of hard-headed dinosaurs, including Pachycephalosaurus, Psittacosaurus, Triceratops, Styracosaurus, and Pachyrhinosaurus.
  ISBN 978-1-60413-403-2
  1. Ornithischia—Juvenile literature. [1. Ornithischians. 2. Dinosaurs.] I. Title. II. Series.
  QE862.O65 B574 2009
  567.914—dc21

                                                        2008000843

Edited by Angelique Campbell-Muir
Illustrations by Nina Sanadze
Page layout by Nina Sanadze

Printed in the United States of America

Acknowledgements
Department of Library Services, American Museum of Natural History (neg. no. PK51), p. 9; Auscape/ John Cancalosi, p. 5, Auscape/Francois Gohier, p. 8 (top), Auscape/Ferrero-Labat, p. 25; Museum Victoria, p. 8 (bottom); © The Natural History Museum, London, p. 17; Getty Images/Photodisc, p.16 (left); Prehistoric Animal Structures, Inc., p. 16 (right); Royal Tyrrell Museum of Palaeontology/Alberta Community Development, pp. 21, 29.

While every care has been taken to trace and acknowledge copyright, the publisher tenders their apologies for any accidental infringement where copyright has proved untraceable.

Contents

Glossary words
When a word is printed in
bold, you can look up its
meaning in the Glossary
on page 31.

Dinosaurs

Dinosaurs lived millions of years ago. Some dinosaurs were huge and others were quite small.

There were many different kinds of dinosaurs.

Many dinosaur bones became buried in the ground. Some turned into rock. Scientists dig up and study these **fossils**.

These dinosaur bones have turned into rock fossils.

Hard Heads

Hard bone covered the heads of some dinosaurs. These hard-headed dinosaurs ate plants.

Triceratops was a hard-headed dinosaur.

Some of these dinosaurs had heads like **helmets**.
Others had **horns**, spikes, or big **frills** made of
bone on their heads.

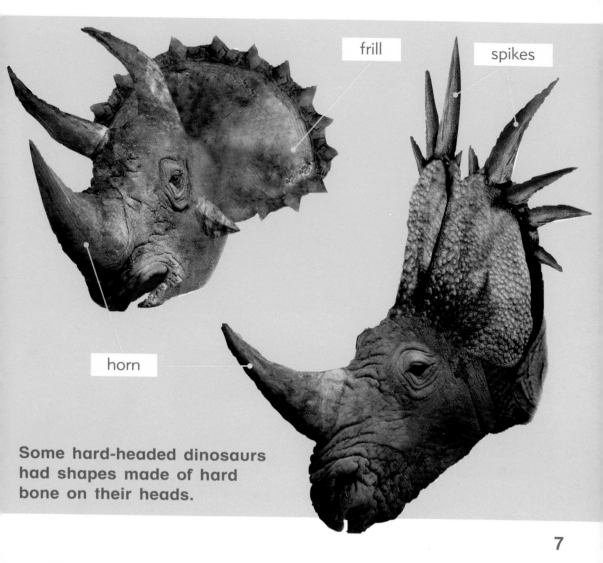

frill

spikes

horn

Some hard-headed dinosaurs
had shapes made of hard
bone on their heads.

The hard-headed dinosaurs had beaks for breaking off plants. They had sharp teeth in their cheeks for cutting up the plants to eat. Their **skulls** show these hard beaks.

This skeleton shows the frill and horns of this hard-headed dinosaur.

Hard-headed dinosaurs had hard beaks with teeth inside.

Hard-headed dinosaurs laid eggs, as all other dinosaurs did. Some eggs did not hatch. Over time they turned into rocks. Scientists have dug up many dinosaur egg fossils.

These dinosaur eggs have been dug up from the ground.

Pachycephalosaurus

(pak-ee-SEF-uh-lo-SAWR-ruhs)

Pachycephalosaurus was not a very big dinosaur. It stood 8 feet (2.4 meters) tall and measured up to 15 feet (4.5 meters) long. Pachycephalosaurus walked on two legs and had a **stiff**, heavy tail.

domed head

Pachycephalosaurus was a dome-headed dinosaur. Very thick bone almost 10 inches (25 centimeters) thick covered the top of its head. Small bony spikes and bumps surrounded the dome.

stiff heavy tail

Pachycephalosaurus was not a very large dinosaur.

Some scientists think the dinosaurs crashed their heads together to fight. Other scientists believe Pachycephalosaurus butted the sides of other animals with its head.

Pachycephalosaurus used their heads to fight.

Pachycephalosaurus had small, sharp teeth in its cheeks. It probably used these teeth to grind soft leaves, fruits, and seeds for food.

Psittacosaurus

(SIT-uh-ko-SAWR-uhs)

Psittacosaurus was a small dinosaur about 4 feet (1 meter) tall. It had a short, boxy head with extra bone at the back. Small horns stuck out of its cheeks.

Psittacosaurus was a small, plant-eating dinosaur.

Psittacosaurus walked and ran on two legs. Its arms were much shorter than its legs.

horn

beak

short arms

Psittacosaurus had a sharp beak similar to a parrot's beak. Psittacosaurus probably used its beak to slice through nuts and other hard plant food. Psittacosaurus also had sharp cheek teeth for cutting up its food.

Psittacosaurus had a similar beak to a parrot.

Psittacosaurus swallowed stones, as many other dinosaurs did. The stones stayed in its stomach to help mash up food.

Stones like these have been found in the stomach of Psittacosauruses.

Triceratops

(try-SAIR-uh-tops)

Triceratops was as heavy as an elephant. It had three horns on its face and a frill of bone at the back of its head.

Triceratops was a large, heavy dinosaur.

Triceratops walked on four strong legs. It had very thick, tough skin. Its large skull was up to 10 feet (3 meters) long.

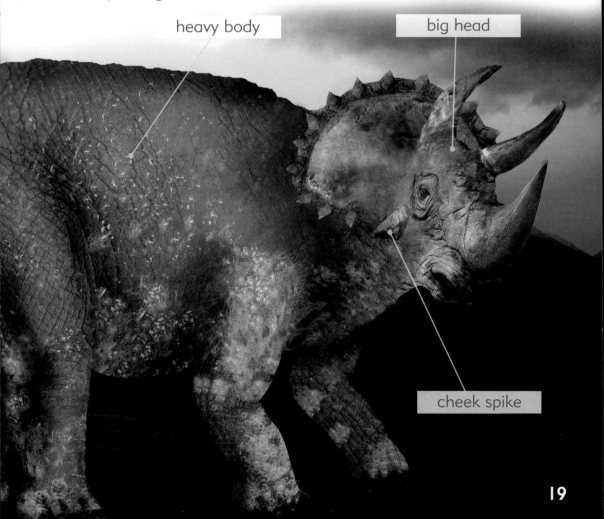

heavy body

big head

cheek spike

Triceratops lived in large **herds**. The herds moved through **woodlands** looking for food. Triceratops used its beak to snip off twigs and leaves to eat.

Triceratops found food in woodlands.

Scientists have dug up many Triceratops bones and studied them. They have put the bones together to make **skeletons**.

This Triceratops skeleton is a fossil made of rock.

Styracosaurus

(stih-RAK-uh-SAWR-uhs)

Styracosaurus had a bulky body, a thick tail, and a large head. It walked on four short legs. Styracosaurus had a horn on its nose that was nearly 2 feet (.6 meters) long.

thick tail

Styracosaurus had a large head with a frill and a long horn.

At the back of its head, Styracosaurus had a frill with six long spikes along the edge. Skin covered the frill.

frill

The frill and spikes protected Styracosaurus from meat-eating dinosaurs. Some scientists think Styracosaurus **charged** at these **predators**.

Styracosaurus used its frill and spikes to protect it from other dinosaurs.

Styracosaurus lived in huge herds, probably in woodlands. The herds walked long distances in search of food. Many animals live in herds today.

Many animals live in herds, just as Styracosaurus used to.

Pachyrhinosaurus

(PAK-ee-rye-no-SAWR-uhs)

Pachyrhinosaurus stood 11 feet (3.5 meters) tall and measured 23 feet (7 meters) long. It had a beak like a parrot's beak to break off palm leaves and other plants to eat.

frill

beak

Pachyrhinosaurus had a large bump of bone on its face. This bone may have been a different shape on males and females. A short frill with two spikes sat at the back of its head.

Pachyrhinosaurus had a short frill and a parrot-like beak.

Males may have fought by crashing the bones on their heads together. They also may have charged at predators to defend themselves.

Pachyrhinosaurus may have used their heads to fight one another.

Scientists have often discovered many Pachyrhinosaurus skeletons together in one place. From these finds, they learned that Pachyrhinosaurus lived in very large herds.

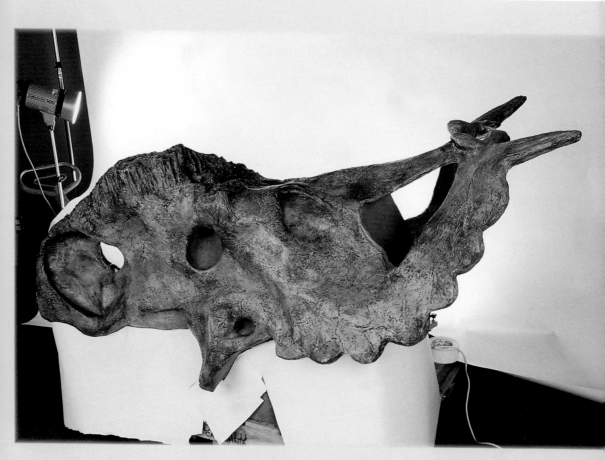

Pachyrhinosaurus skeletons have helped us to learn about the dinosaurs.

Names and Their Meanings

"Dinosaur" means "terrible lizard."

"Pachycephalosaurus" means
"thick-headed lizard."

"Psittacosaurus" means "parrot lizard."

"Triceratops" means "three-horned face."

"Styracosaurus" means "spiked lizard."

"Pachyrhinosaurus" means "thick-nosed lizard."

Glossary

bulky   to be large and take up a lot of space

charge   to rush forward in order to attack

fossil   something left behind by a plant or animal that has been preserved in the earth; examples are dinosaur bones and footprints.

frill   a bony shield on an animal's neck or at the back of the head; frills can be many shapes and sizes.

helmet   a hard covering that protects the head

herd   a large group of animals that live together

horn   a hard, bony growth on the head of an animal; many horns are pointed.

predator   an animal that hunts other animals for food

skeleton   the bones that support and protect an animal's body

skull   the bones of the head

stiff   does not bend

woodland   land covered mainly by trees

Index